P9-BYM-875

DISCARDED

Summit Co. Library System
Kamas Branch
110 No. Main St.
Kamas, Utah 84036
435-783-3190

BOOKWORMS

How It Is Made

Flour to Pasta

B.J. Best

Cavendish
Square

New York

Published in 2017 by Cavendish Square Publishing, LLC
243 5th Avenue, Suite 136, New York, NY 10016

Copyright © 2017 by Cavendish Square Publishing, LLC

First Edition

No part of this publication may be reproduced, stored in a retrieval system, or transmitted in any form or by any means—electronic, mechanical, photocopying, recording, or otherwise—without the prior permission of the copyright owner. Request for permission should be addressed to Permissions, Cavendish Square Publishing, 243 5th Avenue, Suite 136, New York, NY 10016. Tel (877) 980-4450; fax (877) 980-4454.

Website: cavendishsq.com

This publication represents the opinions and views of the author based on his or her personal experience, knowledge, and research. The information in this book serves as a general guide only. The author and publisher have used their best efforts in preparing this book and disclaim liability rising directly or indirectly from the use and application of this book.

CPSIA Compliance Information: Batch #CW17CSQ

All websites were available and accurate when this book was sent to press.

Library of Congress Cataloging-in-Publication Data

Names: Best, B. J., 1976- author.
Title: Flour to pasta / B.J. Best.
Description: New York : Cavendish Square Publishing, [2017] | Series: How it is made | Includes index.
Identifiers: LCCN 2016027441 (print) | LCCN 2016029402 (ebook) | ISBN 9781502621269 (pbk.) | ISBN 9781502621276 (6 pack) | ISBN 9781502621283 (library bound) | ISBN 9781502621290 (ebook)
Subjects: LCSH: Pasta products--Juvenile literature. | Flour--Juvenile literature.
Classification: LCC TP435.M3 B47 2017 (print) | LCC TP435.M3 (ebook) | DDC 664/.755--dc23
LC record available at https://lccn.loc.gov/2016027441

Editorial Director: David McNamara
Copy Editor: Rebecca Rohan
Associate Art Director: Amy Greenan
Designer: Alan Sliwinski
Production Coordinator: Karol Szymczuk
Photo Research: J8 Media

The photographs in this book are used by permission and through the courtesy of: Cover (Flour) Africa Studio/Shutterstock.com, (Pasta) Nosonjai/Shutterstock.com; p. 5 Focal Point/Shutterstock.com; p. 7 AS Food studio/Shutterstock.com; p. 9 ffolas/Shutterstock.com; p. 11 Zigzag Mountain Art/Shutterstock.com; p. 13 Principgalli/iStockphoto.com; p. 15 AGF/UIG/Getty Images; p. 17 AGF/Srl/Alamy Stock Photo; p. 19 Alessia Pierdomenico/Shutterstock.com; p. 21 Hans Neleman/Getty Images.

Printed in the United States of America

Contents

Noodles can be called pasta.

Pasta comes in many shapes.

Macaroni and spaghetti
are pastas.

5

People have eaten pasta for hundreds of years.

It is made around the world.

Pasta is made with flour.

Flour is like a powder.

It is made from **ground** wheat.

At the factory, the flour is stored in **silos**.

11

The flour is mixed with water.

It makes **dough**.

Dough is soft.

13

The dough is pushed through a **die**.

Dies can make different pasta shapes.

15

The fresh pasta dries.

Then long pasta can be cut.

17

The dried pasta is put into boxes or bags.

It is ready to ship to stores.

19

You can buy pasta at the grocery store.

It is **boiled** at home.

Then it is ready to eat!

21

New Words

boiled (BOILED) Cooked in hot water.

die (DIE) Metal that shapes pasta.

dough (DOH) Mixed flour and water.

ground (GROUND) Crushed into powder.

silos (SY-lohs) Large, tall containers.

Index

23

About the Author

B.J. Best lives in Wisconsin with his wife and son. He has written several other books for children. His favorite pasta shape is cavatappi.

About BOOKWORMS

Bookworms help independent readers gain reading confidence through high-frequency words, simple sentences, and strong picture/text support. Each book explores a concept that helps children relate what they read to the world they live in.